Solving Problems at the Zoo

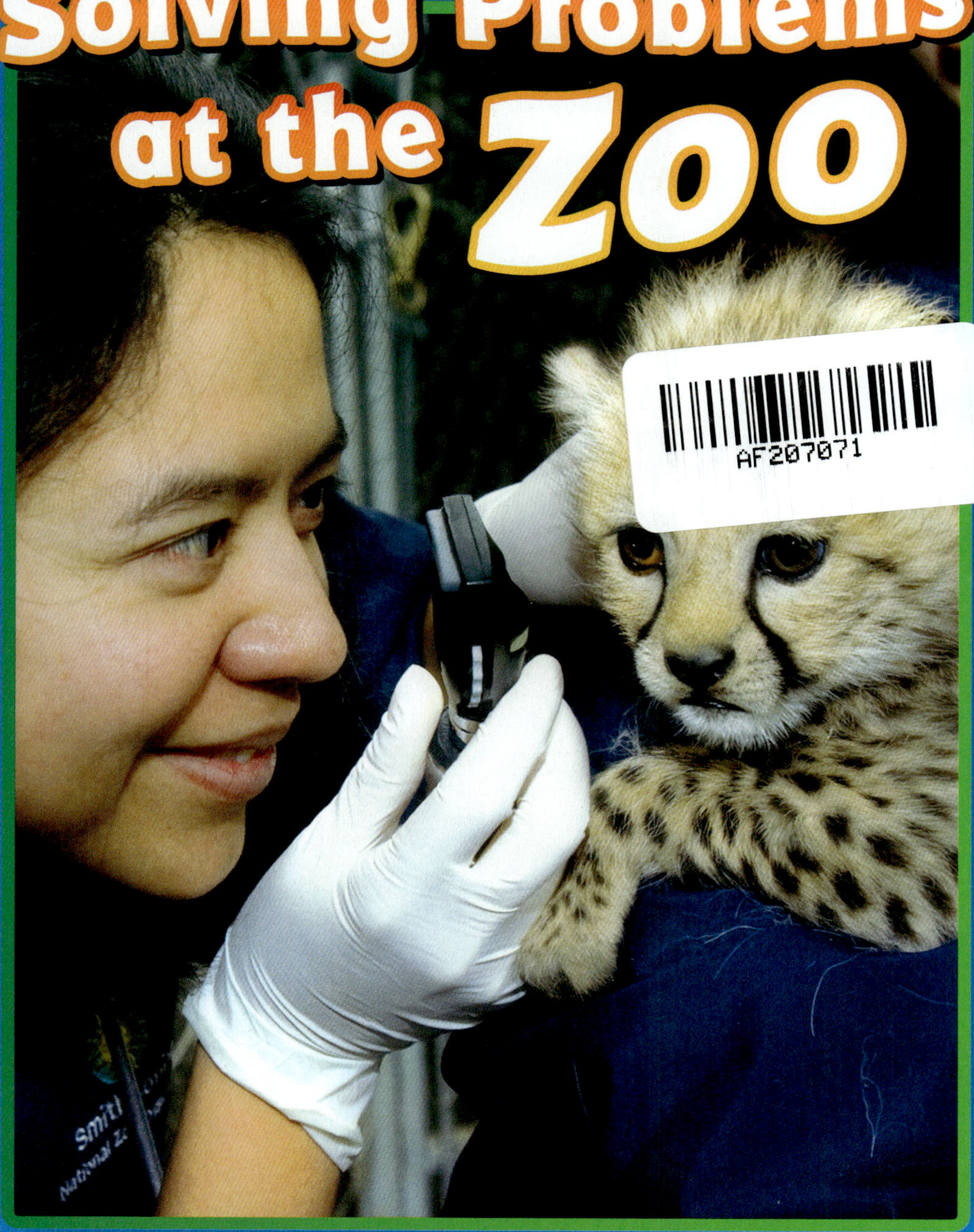

Nellie Wilder

Consultants

Jen Zoon
Communications Specialist
Office of Communications
Smithsonian National Zoo

Amy Zoque
STEM Coordinator and Instructional Coach
Vineyard STEM School
Ontario Montclair School District

Publishing Credits

Rachelle Cracchiolo, M.S.Ed., *Publisher*
Conni Medina, M.A.Ed., *Editor in Chief*
Diana Kenney, M.A.Ed., NBCT, *Series Developer*
Emily R. Smith, M.A.Ed., *Content Director*
Véronique Bos, *Creative Director*
Robin Erickson, *Art Director*
Michelle Jovin, M.A., *Associate Editor*
Mindy Duits, *Series Designer*
Lee Aucoin, *Senior Graphic Designer*
Smithsonian Science Education Center

Image Credits: front cover, p.1, © Smithsonian (photo by Mehgan Murphy); pp.4–12, p.13 (top), p.14 (bottom), p.15, p.16, p.17 (bottom), p.18, p.19, p.22 (top), p.23 (top) © Smithsonian; all other images from iStock and/or Shutterstock.

Library of Congress Cataloging-in-Publication Data

Names: Rice, Dona, author. | Smithsonian Institution, author.
Title: Solving problems as the zoo / Dona Herweck Rice, Smithsonian.
Description: Huntington Beach, CA : Teacher Created Materials, [2020] |
  Audience: K to Grade 3. |
Identifiers: LCCN 2018049793 (print) | LCCN 2018050706 (ebook) | ISBN
  9781493868971 (eBook) | ISBN 9781493866571 (paperback)
Subjects: LCSH: Zoo keepers--Washinton (D.C.)--Juvenile literature. |
  National Zoological Park (U.S.)
Classification: LCC QL50.5 (ebook) | LCC QL50.5 .R53 2020 (print) | DDC
  590.73/753--dc23
LC record available at https://lccn.loc.gov/2018049793

Smithsonian

Teacher Created Materials

5301 Oceanus Drive
Huntington Beach, CA 92649-1030
www.tcmpub.com
ISBN 978-1-4938-6657-1

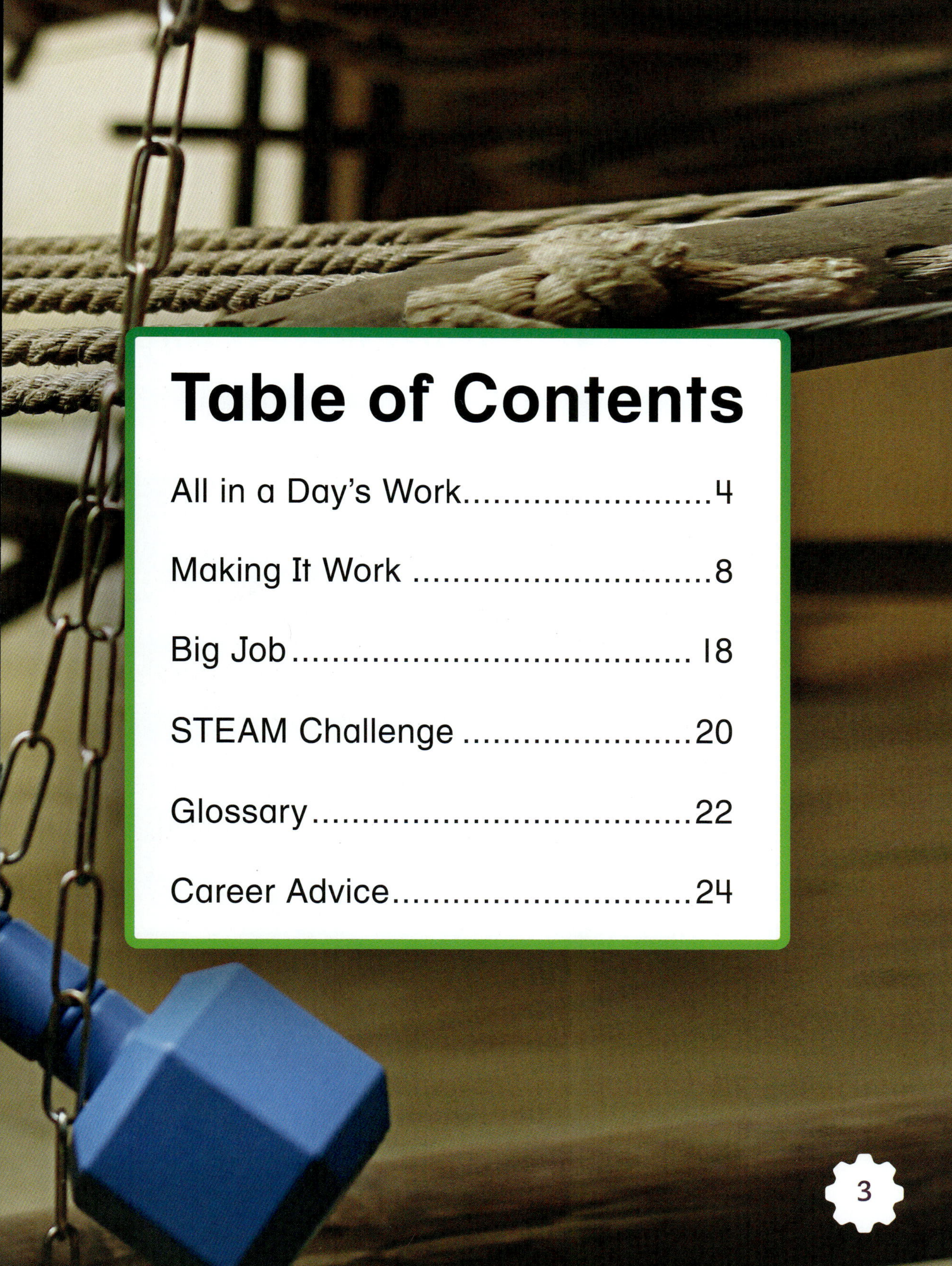

Table of Contents

All in a Day's Work

Life at the Smithsonian's National Zoo is fun! **Keepers** work hard to make it that way.

Keepers gave this tiger a ball to play with.

Bear cubs play at the Smithsonian's National Zoo.

Keepers take care of animals.
They feed them. They keep
them safe. Keepers also
make sure animals have fun!

A keeper brushes
an ape's teeth.

A keeper gives an
alpaca treats while
the alpaca paints.

A keeper trains lemurs to
stand so she can study them.

Making It Work

Keepers face problems each day. They must find the best ways to do their work.

A keeper measures meals for different animals.

A keeper trains a goat to touch a ball so she can check the goat.

Checking Henderson the monkey can be tough. But keepers trained him to come when he sees a ball. That is how keepers talk to him.

A keeper gives Henderson a strawberry as a treat for coming.

Just Right

Temperature in a fish tank must be just right. It is checked first thing each day. Animals can get sick if it is too high or too low.

Keepers also check the birds. They hit a wood block to call them. The sound means breakfast time!

Keepers mix fruit and worms for birds to eat.

A keeper notes which birds come to her after she hits a wood block.

Checking fish can be hard.
Adding **medicine** to the water
helps. It makes the fish go
to sleep.

Keepers use medicine in the
water to make this pacu sleep.

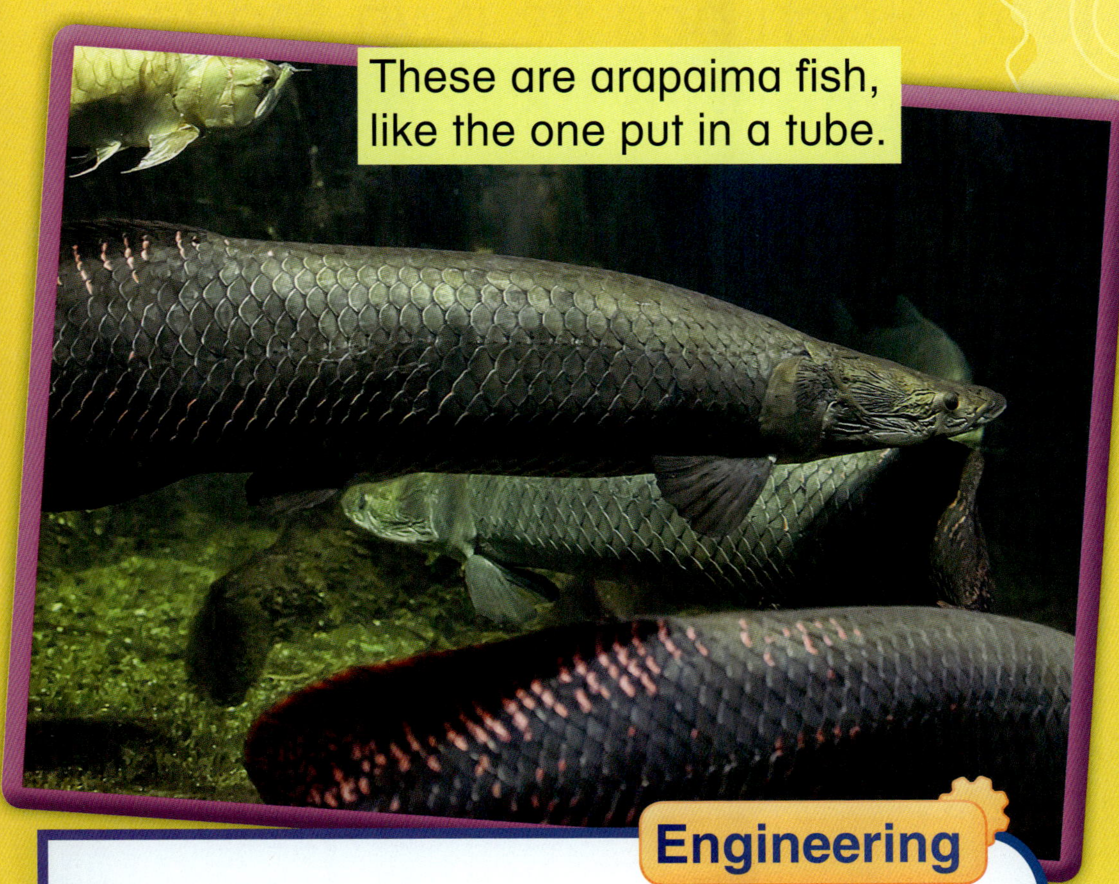

A Fishy Problem

In 2015, keepers had to help a big fish. The fish could hurt them. So, keepers cut slots in a tube. The fish stayed in the tube while they worked on it.

Feeding the animals is a big job! Each has its own foods and **schedule**. Keepers must know them all.

A keeper ties vegetables to wood so the food will sink for the fish.

Zap!

Electric eels may look smooth and soft. But these fish can **shock** keepers! Keepers wear gloves when feeding eels. These special gloves protect keepers from harm.

Big Job

It is a big job to be a good keeper. But the rewards are bigger!

Keepers check the health of a fishing cat kitten.

A keeper rewards alpacas with carrot slices.

STEAM CHALLENGE

The Problem

You and your friend have new jobs at the zoo. You must feed a bird called a finch. Your task is to make a bird-feeding hat. One of you will wear the hat while the other checks the bird!

The Goals

- Design a hat you can wear so that it holds one big spoonful of bird food.
- Design a place on your hat for the finch to land and eat.
- Design a strong enough hat to hold both the bird feed and a coin to represent the finch.

1 Research and Brainstorm

What do finches eat? How much does a finch weigh? What coin is about that same weight?

2 Design and Build

Draw your plan. How will it work? What materials will you use? Make your bird-feeding hat!

3 Test and Improve

Put bird feed in the hat. Add the coin. Does it hold? Does anything fall? Can you make it better? Try again.

4 Reflect and Share

How many finches could you feed on your hat at one time? Is there something else you could make that would be better for feeding and checking a finch?

Glossary

keepers

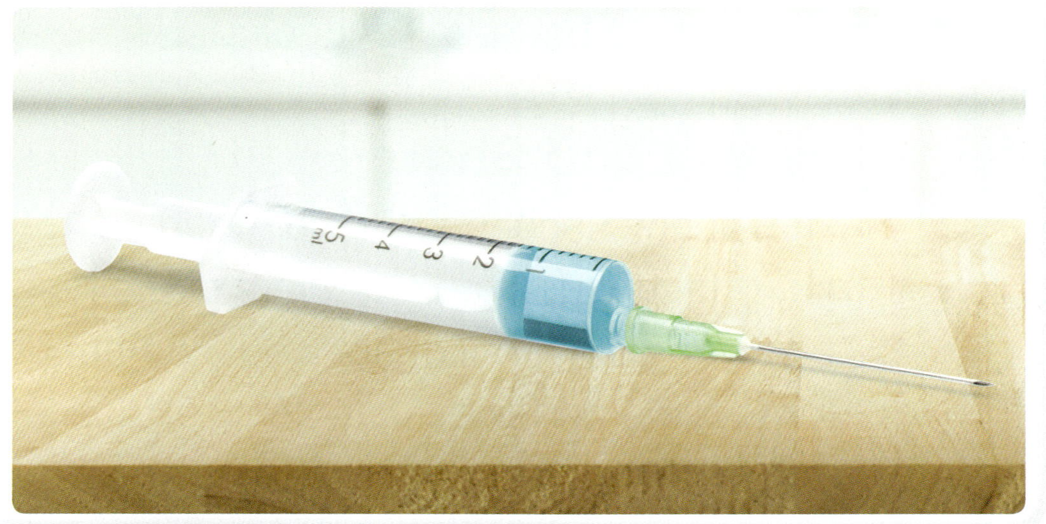

medicine

schedule

shock

temperature

Career Advice
from Smithsonian

Do you want to be a keeper?
Here are some tips to get you started.

"To be a great keeper you have to be curious. You have to work hard and study too."
— Ashton Ball, Small Mammal House Keeper

" When I was young, I fell in love with orangutans. I wanted to teach people about them and how we can save them. So I studied to be a keeper!"
— Kara Ingraham, Small Mammal House Keeper